# The First Americans

## Tribes of North America

*An* I AM READING *Book*

by Jane Werner Watson
pictures by Troy Howell

**PANTHEON BOOKS**

Library of Congress Cataloging in Publication Data.
Watson, Jane Werner, 1915-   The first Americans.
(An *I am reading* book) *Summary:* Easy-to-read text introduces the way
of life of the various groups of native Americans before the arrival
of the white man.   1. Indians of North America—Juvenile Literature.
[1. Indians of North America]   I. Title   E77.4.W27   970.004'97   80-356
ISBN 0-394-84194-8   ISBN 0-394-94194-2 lib.bdg.

Long years ago
in all our wide land
there were no cities.
There were no railways or roads.
There were no horses or wheels.
But there were people living here.

2

3

The people lived in small groups
scattered over the land.
Some wandered across the wide
grassy plains
hunting for food.
They carried their homes—
called *tepees*—with them.
The women and girls of these tribes
could set up the tepees quickly.

The men hunted wild buffalo.
The people ate the meat of the buffalo.
They wore its hide for clothing.
They covered their tepees
with buffalo hide.
The men made tools from buffalo bones.
No wonder these tribes came to be known
as the people of the buffalo!

Winters were hard on the plains.
The people set up camps
close to rivers.
Some heaped earth
around the bottom
of their tepees.
Others built lodges of earth
to keep out the winter winds.
Often there was not much food.

Boys were sent out alone at night
to fetch water.
Or they spent days and nights alone
without food or water
to test their bravery.
Boys of the plains tribes wanted to
grow up to be good hunters and warriors.

They learned to make
war whistles, war clubs,
and bows and arrows.
They also learned to shape
bowls for pipes from stone
and to make stems from wood.
A boy started work
as a moccasin-bearer
or as a servant to a warrior.
Then he became a water-carrier.
After that he scouted
for herds of buffalo
and kept an eye out for enemies.
If he was a good scout
he became a warrior.
The best warrior became the chief.

For play, the boys wrestled
or rolled small hoops with spears.
They spun tops and played stick ball.
Their balls were made of deer or
buffalo hair wrapped in strips of hide.
Girls played house with toy tepees
or carried puppies on their backs
instead of baby dolls.
And they helped their mothers.

East of the Mississippi River
most of the land
was covered with great forests.
Many animals lived in the forests—
bear and woodland buffalo and deer.
The men of the woodland tribes
hunted these animals for food
for their families.

They also hunted smaller animals—
rabbit, beaver, opossum, squirrel,
and wild turkey.
Boys of these tribes
learned to move silently
through the forest
so they could be good hunters.
The men and boys also cleared trees
and burned bushes.

In these clearings, the women and girls
raised corn and beans and squash.
They also gathered fruits and nuts
and grass seeds and bulbs
that were good to eat.
In the fall, children gathered
walnuts, hickory nuts, and acorns
in the woods.

The woodland people
liked to live together in villages.
In summer many of them moved to
summer homes near a lake or stream.
They caught fish, turtles, and shellfish.
When water birds flew south in the fall,
the men caught some of them for food.
Usually there was plenty to eat
in the woods.

Homes were made of poles
covered with bark or mud or grass mats
to keep out the harsh weather.
Some of them were round.
They were called *wigwams* or *wickiups*.
Other tribes built long houses
in which many families lived together.

Each family had its own cooking-fire
and a space for a sleeping-shelf.
In the cold winters
people had more time to work indoors.
They made fur robes and leggings and
moccasins trimmed with porcupine quills.
They made smoking pipes and tools,
and decorations of shell beads.

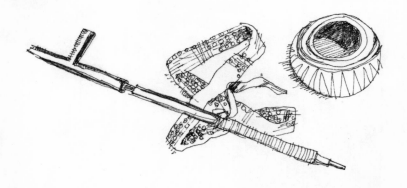

The women wove baskets out of grass
and made boxes and pots of birchbark.
Canoes were often made of birchbark, too.

17

While the families worked,
the old people told stories—
about the Great Spirit
who watched over them from the sky,
about the Sun which gave them life,
about the Thunderbird who
roared from the clouds during storms

and the animals which gave them food—
and about the heroes of their people.
Some tribes made mounds of earth
in the shape of snakes, eagles,
wildcats, and other animals
for which they had special respect.
Grass grew over these mounds
and some can still be seen today.

Paths led through the woodlands.
Sometimes people of other tribes
came along those paths to trade furs,
grain, or hard stone for arrow points.
Many of the tribes used strings
of shell beads called *wampum*
to pay for things
they bought.

Tribes spoke different languages.
But they could speak together
in sign language.
Some Indians in the woodlands
had fur and wild rice to trade.
They did not raise crops.
They were hunters and fishermen.

In the snowy winters
they walked over the thick, soft snow
on snowshoes.
They pulled their wares on toboggans.
Suits of furry hides kept them warm.

North of the woods,
on the icy treeless plains, or *tundra*,
other hunters and fishermen lived.
They went to sea in skin boats
to hunt whale, seal, and fish.
On land they traveled in sleds
pulled by husky dogs.

There were no trees
to give them poles or bark
for their homes.
So they made houses of snow
or chunks of earth rounded at the top
over rafters of curved whale bone.

In the long dark winters
they sat on their sleeping-shelves
inside their warm sod or snow houses.
They burned whaleblubber for light.
Often they did not have much food.

The women and girls worked
at softening hide for clothing
by chewing it.
The men and boys
carved tools and decorations
from stone, ivory, or bone.
And the old people told stories.

South of the icy tundra,

near the Pacific Ocean,

deep forests grew.

Tribes in these forests fished

and gathered shellfish from the sea.

In the spring

they went out in big canoes

to hunt giant gray whales.

In the summer

the woods gave them berries and fruit.

This rich land could feed many families,

so people lived in large villages.

In the rainy, stormy winters

they lived in the shelter of the forests.

In spring and summer

they paddled their canoes

down the coast to summer homes.

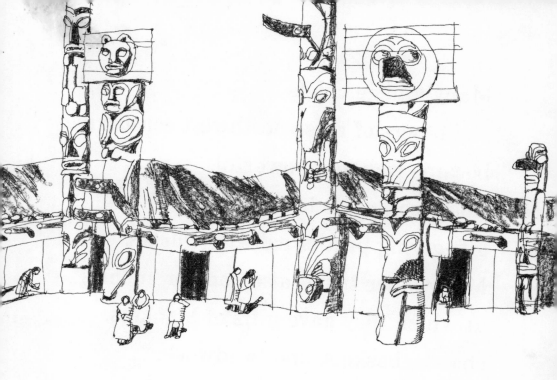

They built sturdy wooden houses
with posts carved
from soft, tall cedar trees.
Their canoes were made from cedar logs.
And they carved tall poles
into the shapes of the animals
their families felt related to—
deer, bear, turtle, beaver, or eagle.

Many village chiefs

and others of these northwest coast tribes

became rich and powerful.

They took pride in having

gift-giving parties called *potlaches.*

Many other tribes also had ceremonies

at which they gave gifts of blankets,

shawls, baskets, and beadwork.

The gifts honored those who got them.

They also showed how rich the giver was.

Sometimes in one great party

a rich man of the northwest coast

gave away all he owned!

Of course he would soon be invited

to someone else's potlach

and be given fine gifts in return.

31

Parties, festivals, music, and dancing
were very important
to these people of long ago.
At the center of almost any village
was an open space for dancing.
All year there were sun dances,
rain dances, corn dances, deer dances,
harvest dances, and winter dances.

Every tribe had its own special dances.
There were special dances
to honor young people,
both boys and girls,
as they grew up.

Often dancers wore costumes.
They wore masks
to honor a spirit or god.
And as a man danced,
he seemed to become that spirit.
To make music,
people beat on painted drums,
shook rattles made of dry gourds,
and blew into whistles or pipes.
Some of the best dances
were those of the southwest tribes
who lived in bare, dry country
where it was often very hot.

Some of the people of the southwest
made simple shelters
of thin posts or logs
covered with brush or clay.
But many tribes
built towns of high-piled houses
made of stone or sun-dried brick.

Usually the town was built

on top of a cliff

or into the side of one, for protection.

It was often a long climb

to the town's small fields.

There was little rain.

Water for the corn, beans, and squash

had to be brought from streams

and pools by digging ditches.

Small boys and girls had long walks, too,
taking the family flocks to pasture.
These children of long ago
had to learn
to live with heat and cold,
rain, snow, and hunger.
If sickness came
a medicine man was called.

He brought herbs to cure the sickness
or he called on good spirits to help.
A sand painting could bring the spirits.

People of long ago
lived close to the spirits
of the earth and air
and sea and sky.
They believed that the land and waters
belonged to everyone—
to use and to enjoy—
and to pass on to their children.

It was nearly five hundred years ago
when sailing ships
started to cross the ocean
to this wide land.
People of other lands saw
the deep forests, the swift rivers,
the grassy clearings.
They liked what they saw
and wanted it for themselves.

41

2

More and more of them came,
bringing horses, wheels, guns,
and many new ways of living.
Since then life has never been the same
for the tribes of the first Americans.

JANE WERNER WATSON has written over two hundred books for children. She was born in Wisconsin and began her career as an editor and a staff writer for Golden Press. She has been a freelance writer since 1954, and in 1958 the *Los Angeles Times* named her Woman of the Year for Literature. Under the name of W.K. Jasner, she wrote the spooky and popular I AM READING Book, *Which is the Witch?* Her hobbies are traveling and photography. She lives in Santa Barbara, California.

TROY HOWELL always knew he would be an artist. He taught himself to draw when he was a boy, and his first illustrating job was for *Cricket* magazine. Since then he has created pictures for many children's books. His drawings for *The First Americans* are done in pen and crayon, and the cover is a combination of acrylic paint and pencil. He was born in Long Beach, California, in 1953 and later went to classes at the Art Center School in Los Angeles. He now lives in Fredericksburg, Virginia, with his wife and small son.